MW00846816

TARGET POPULATIONS

TARGET POPULATIONS

MARC KAMINSKY

CENTRAL PARK EDITIONS
1991

Many of these poems were previously published in magazines. I want to thank the editors of ***Central Park*** ("Defense," "Anyone," "Broker"), ***Social Text*** ("Screens," "Breaking the Glass," "Job Society"), ***Hunter Magazine*** ("Walkman," "Watch Repairman"), ***New York Quarterly*** ("Shelterless"), ***Israel Horizons*** ("Black Cat"), and ***Socialist Review*** ("The Lighthouse Keepers," a long poem that was originally part of this book, had to be cut here for lack of money/space).

ISBN: 0-9622390-2-X
First Edition

Library of Congress Card Catalogue Number: 91-071790

Cover Photograph: Neil Wexler
Production: Margaret Styne and Stephen-Paul Martin

Central Park Editions
Box 1446
New York, New York 10023

ACKNOWLEDGMENTS

This book is dedicated to Alan Feldman. For many years, his meticulous, empathic, problem-posing readings of my unpublished poems have been vital in sustaining a collegial context that, for poets, in the absence of any actual community, is so necessary and so keenly appreciated.

I want also to thank the other writers and friends who were important to me in completing this book. I mean not only that they received the writing, but that they offered back useful criticism and embedded the writing of poetry in ordinary relationships of shoptalk and support. This ongoing dialogue included Allan Appel, Stanley Aronowitz, Dennis Bernstein, Sara Blackburn, Eve Ensler, Polly Howells, Stephen-Paul Martin, Bill McClellan, Diane Meier, Bill Packard, Dennis Nurkse, Rochelle Ratner, Steve Schrader, Rima Shore, Arthur Strimling, Margo Viscusi, Mark Weiss and Eric Werthman. Maddy Santner's commitment to my writing life has shaped my immediately happy working conditions.

Target Populations is the second volume of a two-part work titled ***In the Traffic of a Targeted City.*** This book and the first volume, ***The Road from Hiroshima,*** comprise the text of a theater piece that was presented at the Theater for the New City in May, 1986. With music by Steve Browman, and acted by Diane Dowling and Athur Strimling (who also directed the work), it has been performed throughout Europe and the United States. The following poems were part of the text of the theater piece: "Rapid Shifts in Position," "The Green Woman," "Walkman," "Grotto," "Watch Repairman." Dennis Bernstein produced an earlier version of this piece for National Public Radio, which won the Art of Peace Award in 1983.

In "Screens," the argument concerning the discontinuity between the viewer and the photographed moment is taken from John Berger's essay, "Photographs of Agony," in ***About Looking,*** pp. 37-40.

These poems were written between 1981 and 1985, except for "Bad Air," which was written in the first days of the Gulf War.

Contents

I. Disturbed Relations

II. Curriculum Vitæ

I. Disturbed Relations

Defense

Blackout of the Architect Joe Stylianos

1.

This again? A red light
on the corner where Houston
meets the Bowery, the girls'
legs sheathed in tights

the color of gun barrels

the men on traffic islands
are each a John
barefoot and cursing in the name
of a private Jesus.

2.

A young one
with a sculptured mane of gray hair
points us out menacingly

his bare skin under a suit jacket
looks like the slabs of sheet rock
that leap at the eye—chalky

and blotched, exposed in half-
torn tenement walls
that hang in the air like washing

Delirium tremens
is showing him something terrible
to look at

He follows its course
his whole body drawn upward
by what he sees

drifting over the roofs toward Avenue A

he shrieks, hides his face
glares at us

curls back his lips

approaches

and spits out the prophetic
words we can't hear—

our windows rolled up.

3.

You and I stare
as if we see nothing but congestion of molecules
in immobilized air

the light over the city
is plaster

Towers
rise before us like columns
on the front
page of *The New York Times:*
a layout
whose verticality suddenly fails
to give me a lift

and litter of newsprint
doesn't rise
and fall like a sheet
under which the street is still breathing

We're suffocating

under this hardened sky
on this papered earth

we haven't spoken
a word to each other
for hours.

4.

Stuck here, afraid
he is going to hurl a brick
through the windshield

enraged
that you have gone into the bleak mood
where I can't break through

left alone with my violence

I steal away from the surfaces
of my body
the way old people do.

5.

And I sit
amid all the ages of my life

powerful in my cage of bones

a walled city I retreat to

hidden by branches of lung
and a mess of intestines

no one

will get me

6.

Here in this interior city
things are now clear to me—

we will not be saved.

7.

This is the dead
feeling that always comes back

between me
and the women I've tried

to live with
there's this cloud

in which I see
you disappear

8.

And I watch your stony face
dissolve

like white and gray dots
of newspaper face
growing enlarged, breaking
loose

from the shapes that contain
them, and the drunk
who ran at the car
and the hood of the car

dissolve

and the rows of windows
and the dark rooms inside
and the rooms with one naked
light bulb and the girls

exploding
out of their tank tops
and the bodies
of men lying in doorways—

particles of dust

streaming
and darkening around me

the whole city floating
imageless around me

a cloud of dust

like the spill of coherence
out of the shapes
of things

just before I lose
consciousness

9.

I'm seized
by a terror that's never real

until the assurance
that New York's skyline normally gives me
dissolves

as if the great wall of skyscrapers
were a hero's shield

and all the crowding sidestreets of America
were holding it up
to intimidate the ocean

now it rushes in

Anyone

I'm straw and anything
gets me going anyone's
glance ass thigh jeans
tight over crotch

skin tight shirts breasts
with sharp nipples three
and four times a day
in rest rooms anyone

can have me I
let them do anything
they want
on the tiles behind

the door of a coin-drop
toilet in the arcades
in back of concrete piles
on piers at the movies

between classes at work
I'm not
a boy or girl I'm whatever
they want to make me.

After you put your tongue
in someone's anus
you're free
to be anything

with the hands tied
with a candle
dropping hot wax
on the skin with a hood

with pins with words
till the blood comes
and I'm anyone and anyone
has me in flames.

Shelterless

The Woman with Ulcerated Legs

1.

Thievy hotels! You hear the works
clinking behind the wall.
They're shooting up in the bathroom.

You ball up under the blanket.
And listen: someone
is getting murdered in the hallway.

No locks anywhere! You
pray none of those junkies will walk through the door.
They won't stop at anything.

Bad lays! Layers of stain!
Scabies you can't get rid of!
Mattress smell like a sewer!

Even if no one touches you
you lie down with filth.
One time they tied me down there

with pieces of dog leash.
Three days! And every hour
someone else walks in

and takes what he wants from me.
Whatever they wanted.
And when they finished with me and

let me go
I was tired. Just tired.
I'm not stopping anywhere now.

2.

Here it's the cops' turn.
They thwack you.
On the soles. With night sticks.

They have laws
against your sleeping
in the same position they do.

So you steal 15-20 minutes
at Burger King. Sitting upright.
That's the limit.

Someone whose job is
to take your shoulder
and shake it

till your head comes off
the table is
doing his job

everywhere! whether they
whack you or attack you nicely—
what does it matter?

No one
is going to let you stretch out
and rest.

Never again
are you going to get a good night
of rest.

This is what hell is.
You can't believe tiredness like this
can exist you can't

believe how so much
heaviness can be
in one body

and how you carry it
around is beyond
anything you walk

in a haze you can't
help staggering people
take you for drunk

days and nights—all one
scraping against the eye
with a sandpapery lid

the head reeling
for the next place
to touch down.

3.

Five a.m., on my way
to church
where they hand out rolls and coffee

I stumbled
and fell asleep on the street
where I landed.

I must have been walking
for three days.
Look at these legs!

I'm going to keep that
good clean patch
of sunlight on them forever.

Screens

for John Berger

Between panic
and stupor

I'm hurtled along the same lines
as everyone else
                    commuting

between grief
and helplessness

reading the newspapers
                    flipping
through magazines in the dead time

between trains
and terminals

pictures that give us our daily shot
of fire and
flood

and half-naked bodies liquidated
by professionals
                    small doses

of the end of the world

innoculate us

•

And
pictures of splendid athletes
in training
semi-nude, giants, all stress
and discipline
or punishing each other
with a violence that dazzling control
makes exquisite,
speed, and skill, and a tremendous will

to endure
and something unexpected
become visible
in the leap
to score, the ethereal
catch
the shock that fells
a powerful fighter—
our true saints!

they perform the only miracles
we believe in
and we shall meet them again
after their winning
careers, holding up
labor-saving devices
on the subway
selling bank accounts
on the bus

•

a glimpse
of the parts
of the bodies of women

on magazine racks

from lifesize posters on subway walls
        a leg
                shooting out
as the crowd parts
        a hip
                jutting toward you

and the model depicted behind the stop-and-start
        lines of assembled passengers
                appears to be moving
abruptly
        like the women on the platform
                and the women on the platform
seem duplicated
        so many times
                they collapse

into the face of a single woman
        who gives you the feeling
                she sees you
and her fabulous existence
        will one day be yours
                if only you would look at things
the way she does:
        one hand on her hip
                the other holding a dog-
headed walking stick
        as she advances in a soldierly pose—
                a conqueror
reviewing
        all those who pass below
                her unmoved eyes

•

A woman falls to her knees.
Her arms thrown into the air.

Beside her, a girl
stares into the camera.

Behind her, a man sprawls
on the road. He looks dead.

There is nothing else in the picture
but the refugees' handcart

and a few mounds of charred wood
where a village was fire-bombed.

Then you turn the page. But
wait! something is happening

that you've lived through
before—something

weird—turn back and
catch it! Catch it! So

the man is wearing a t-shirt.
The woman is entirely in the scream

she is trying to reach the sky
with. Only her body falls.

Her arms raise up an endless cry.
The child watches you

with the blank eyes of a
child

in the face of.... All this
taking its course again

All-too-familiar, reach me!
Tell me what's going on!

Then for the first time
you saw it: the heart

of this encounter lies
in its impossibility.

No matter how you strain
you will not hear her scream.

And that was the clue.
That was how I began

to understand the whole
process. As you emerge

from the isolation
of the photographed moment

you see only your own
discontinuity

from the family's suffering,
not the frame of double

violence, the gun and the camera
that shoot them

that set them apart. Disrupted
simulacra, these are

figures who don't participate
in the actual

lives of the people in the
photograph, or in yours—

but how quickly you feel
that you alone are responsible

for this absence of a real
connection. And you're shocked.

Not by the actions of men
in power, but by your lack

of a good response. Then after
the soul has its cry

and hands that would staunch
the blood and bathe the wounds

go back to their pockets
and a token

is dropped into the turnstile,
the new perspective

and the vertigo of empathy
don't pass quickly enough.

And you are oppressed
by questions. But what

can you do? How does one
enter the picture?

So you return to the task
at hand—as return you must—

estranged from your life
and estranged, equally,

from the possibilities that begin
in estrangement, disqualified,

compassion turning into self-
contempt, which turns

to numbness, from which you turn
to things that can shock,

give back the sensation
of life. So turned

and turned again, you can
tell yourself you are choosing

to "play the game" of
blind man's buff, or

you can enter
the confrontation

that the moment of frozen agony
masks: what is missing

in your life (in my life) are the organs
of popular power

that can intervene to protect
this family: to govern

the force used in our name:
to stop the bombing.

But then, just as I was following
this train of thought

between denial and dissidence—
in preparation for my talk

on images that screen
our despair—I saw

the old man of the subways
who works the D train

between Coney Island
and Times Square

take off his shoes,
ceremoniously bundle them

in the blanket he wears,
place the bundle at his feet

and begin to preach. I knew
as well as he that we're living

"in the first circle
of the zone of lethality,"

but I was running
late for my lecture, as usual

as I hurried by, I
felt nothing but irritation.

The Writers

To Name Opposing Desires

Revenge

Blade breaks into the train yard
And commits a work of art.
At dawn, bursting cars will become
A traveling exhibition.

Ambition

No one will keep Sly locked in the slums.
The train that takes him nowhere
Will bear his name
From Utica Avenue to Woodlawn Cemetery.

Collective Imagery

It all got started where Ace
And the other writers hung out:
Their invention of happiness
First took place among advertisements.

Expropriation

Faze III takes all the property
With his famous style.
Highways, high-rises, hospitals, subways—
The bubble letters claim all of it.

Walkman

1.

In History
the teacher asked us:
how do you prepare
for nuclear war?
Can it be done?
He divided the class

into two teams
and had us debate
the issue.
At the end we voted.
Mostly everyone
voted no.

2.

And my heart
was racing
so fast I didn't think
I'd be able to
talk
maybe what I wanted

to say
was stupid
but how could they
raise their arms
and vote no
so calmly?

3.

Listen, I said,
I made a tape
exactly 26 minutes long
it took me weeks
to pick the top 8 songs
of my life.

I'll tell you something
I cried
when I had to leave out
"Saturday Night Fever."
But there just wasn't time
for everything.

I got in a few good licks
though. And I carry this
tape with me everywhere.
So people can prepare
and they do, everyone
does in his own way.

4.

When the warning comes
I'll put on my headphones
and turn on
my tape
and let the music blast off

let it take my mind
off the earth
and go to my feet
and I'll just start walking on air
till I meet the bomb.

Watch Repairman

1.

Even now
I don't know what to do
about them:

my wife
who couldn't abandon
her furniture

my son
determined to finish his book
on Wagner

Father couldn't believe
the ministers in black leather
were death

my friend
who buried his circumcised dread
in the little hours you rent in hotel rooms

and I
who found the consolations of daily life
insufficient, I alone

survived.

2.

There were heroes: first
and foremost were those with the courage
to see in time.

I was not with them. Blinded
by humility. Or what I once called humility.
And by love. Or what passed

in our world for love. My attachment
to those who looked at the mask of evil
and called it a human face.

I thought: Who are you
to move against the weight
of their judgment?

And I thought: You will be crushed.
I thought: Who
will listen to you?

And even if
your nightmares are the real
news

who
will repair the damage if you
awaken the sleepwalkers?

So when the officials told us
to pack our bags
and come to the terminal

I, too,
took my place
quietly, in line.

3.

No one told us: no

not the shoes you wore
to the state opera house

but the old boots
in back of the closet—

and even then
you probably won't survive.

Here retired admirals
speak against the arms race.

Scientists proclaim their warnings
on television.

You ask: how could we
go to our deaths like sleepwalkers?

But you of all people
should not ask.

Broker

1.

Last night she said: Tell me
can you explain the way
we get so tired?

She said: Why don't you just come
inside me? And I did. In three seconds
it was over. And I was glad.

Sometimes we go for weeks
without missing
what we both used to die for.

2.

And now this morning
the knot in my stomach is lateness:
the late train nowhere in sight
I lean over the edge of the platform, looking

for oncoming lights. Not there.
The anger is rising:
at my back I hear the hiss
of my boss putting the brakes on

his fury. Later and later.
Can't help it. I even left a half-
hour earlier. What more can I do?
Pace up and down, working

a head of rage, like the crazies
who curse whatever's in front of them
and behind them: slowdown
and speed-up: train and boss:

squeezed inbetween, who can I be
angry with? where can I go
with this? And the day's just beginning.
Near the yellow line

you feel the pressure of each
passing minute in the bodies
that crowd against one another
three deep, then four, then five

more weight, and then more, waiting
to push through the half-opened doors with arms
half-fallen asleep. This is it.
Something rumbling in the distance

fills the whole station: a wild
tremor passing through the crowd
will set it in motion. Now. All breathing
stops. And the wrong train thunders in.

This is the stuff
my heart attack will be made of:
the administration of such little shocks:
the wheels grinding against the rails

shriek: stop it! Just as my F enters.
Relief. Then annoyance. I see
that it's mobbed. As I rush
forward behind a slowmoving overcoat

it's hard to hold down
the hands that want to shove her
aside, the eyes that observe
my contortions offend me.

We crawl on neglected tracks
toward Manhattan. By the time
I get to the office
I'll be ready for violence.

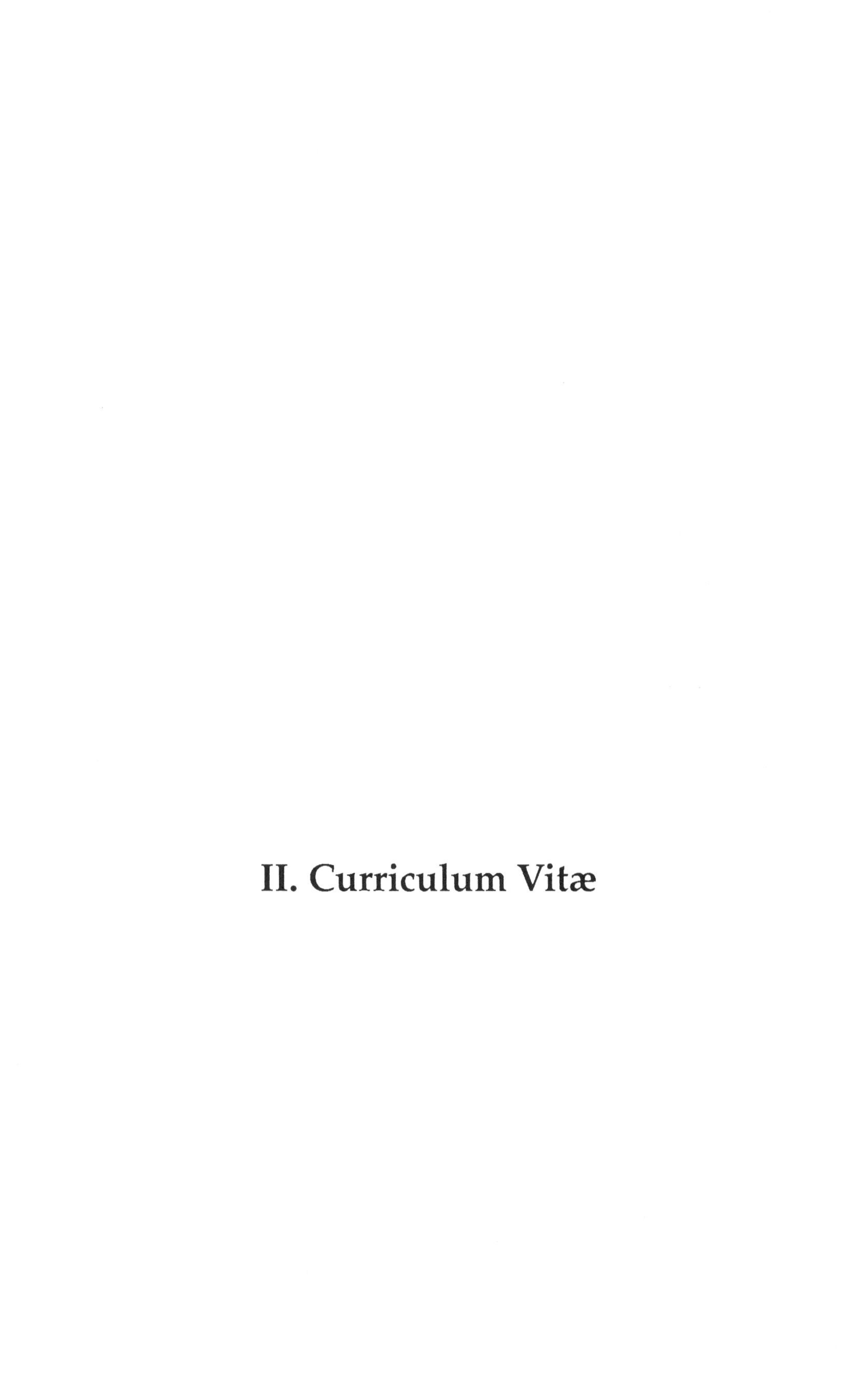

II. Curriculum Vitæ

Rapid Shifts in Position

Vita: of M.K.

1. Street Games

Born in 1943.
Grew up in the traffic
of a targeted city.

With chalk. And asphalt.
Home and second
base were manhole

covers. He played
in the intervals
between oncoming cars.

2. Talisman

At school, acquired
the basic skills.
And a stainless steel

chain around the neck.
He learned: this
was a first acquisition

of status.
And he learned:
it is the necklace

that soldiers wear
into battle. He loved
its silveriness

and the clattering
sound of running
the name plate

along its string
of tiny
ball bearings. He

put them into his mouth
and pulled them taut
like a horse's bit.

A nervous habit.
His teachers
tried to break him

of this. So he started
to finger his chain
as if it were both

his rosary
and his worry beads.
No one explained it

to him. But he knew:
his name
and his charred remains

could be separated
and thanks
to the dog tag

he would be sent
to the correct parents
for burial.

3. Alarms

Starting in 1953:
was schooled in the traffic
of a targeted city.

With gongs. And drills.
Buildings were marked
with signs to the A-bomb

shelters. He thrived
in the intervals
between oncoming wars.

Grotto

I remember how hushed the room was
we were taken by surprise
every time
she whispered it breathlessly—
"Take cover!"

and we dove into a cave
of arms, our own
and those of our desk-chairs—
two virginal bodies in the fifth grade
huddled side by side

I in my red-knit tie, my white shirt
and blue pants, all dressed
for assembly
and you were a long-legged girl
in a sailor's outfit

I already loved
your burning eyes and dark complexion
and your straight black hair
fell across my arm
I knew you had nothing on

under your dress
when you rubbed against me, the skin
of your arm and thigh
brushed against me
and a sheet of flame ran across my skin!

Oh air raid drills of the early fifties!
sublime minutes
when Linda Brandon and I
floated in never-known-before darkness
our refuge

from flying-cloud-mushroom-glass magic—
immersed
in the violence of opposing feelings—
something burst
and flooded my chest—

a delicious sensation
of safety—
my joints suddenly frozen—my legs ached
with cold—no longer in control
of my trembling muscles

for a whole year too frightened to move
while you and I were hidden
from everyone's eyes, with our eyes
closed—my first taste
of romantic love

and the little hours
of the flesh in anguish, rushing
toward dissolution
in the world-annihilating body
of Linda—

not ten feet from the loudspeaker

The Green Woman

for Diane Meier

For a long time I wondered:
what is to be done?
The time given to me on earth
is already half gone

I have little to waste
on public causes
and I dislike the righteous ones
who wave aside my nuances.

Look, I told them, I am
an artist. I meant:
my days are eaten up
with putting bread on the table

my nights with putting on paper
what my life has given me
to make known, my friends
complain they don't see me

enough, and I also yearn
for them, and a few hours
of ceasing to drop
through these bottomless weeks

in this speeded-up, well-planned
rampantly efficient absence
of time, where will I fit
more tasks? how can I commmit

more hours
than I've been given to work with?
And the woman chairing
this committee of six artists

each of whom also had
bread to put on the table
images to get out of the head
and onto the page

this woman
who had similarly complained
and similarly walked out ot meetings
stood up impatiently and said:

I don't know how many nights
I lay awake with an aching conscience—like you
I wasted days, months, asking:
what is to be done?

We have a hall to rent. Posters
to print. Money to raise.
Come back when you are tired
of being agitated.

As I got up to leave the room
she added: And don't think
I'm promising you peace
of mind. The exhilaration

of working to save the planet
will pass quickly enough.
Immersed in routine tasks, you
won't feel particularly ennobled.

Nor will you feel despairing.
You will simply know: you
are doing what must be done.
But this will be enough

to allow you to remain fully conscious—
even of the anguish at the bottom
of oceans
in these deadening times.

Black Cat

for Maddy Santner

1.

And I thought only of driving her out
Of our yard. With a broom.
Or a bucket of water.
And it was already pouring.

But you,
Agitated, worried about her, actually called her
A person. And you said,
"I feel like a murderer."

So to spare you
I climbed out on to the fire escape.
And found her. Under the beam
Of my flashlight. As if speared

She tried to move back into the darkness.
Silent at last. Last night
She had been only a night-long scream
Of pain. Silenced now.

So I kept
My searchlight trained on her cringing body
As she crawled out of her dry spot,
Made a few tries at walking

Through the barred basement window,
Bunched herself into an arched heap,
Then ceased
To try anything....

If I committed an act
Of kindness, it doesn't matter—
I, who thought only of getting
A good night's sleep—

And I thought: it's a good thing
I've never been truly tested.
Lord knows what I'd be capable of
Making my peace with.

2.

But you! So exposed
To an uncloudlike conscience—
You can't even let a sick stray be sick
Under your window, without feeling responsible.
It gives me no comfort to know this:

You are loyal to something
That lets others believe life is to be
Clung to, no matter what the cost. Only you
Get no benefit by feeling
What wretches feel.

In the unguaranteed life in which I deal
And am surprised a little
Each day I find my whole enterprise
Still hasn't collapsed,
Of you I am certain:

In the cities
Where the audible tortured cries
Are human
You would be among those
Who don't survive.

Breaking the Glass

It is the beginning of a dance.
The heel that shall trample the serpent's head
Enters the Second Temple

As its stones are shattered, as if
They are glass; doors of the ark,
Not guarded by rock,

Guard our prayers from bombardment.
They are crushed in an instant.
The words are ended.

And we are not in Jerusalem.
Or Warsaw. Babi Yar is not
One place, but many, in Central

America, this is happening now:
Tongues of fire
That have been made to disappear

Out of mouths that subverted
The First, and the Second World, and the Third
Return, they are here and breathing

Our air. We hear boots stamping out
Memories against cobblestones.
Thus the ceremony ends

With éclat: it breaks the hush
Of that ritual and signals the onset
Of the real

In which we witness this marriage:
This act in which we take our place
In the bodies of a bride and groom

And begin again, in the service
Of what is ours and all creation's.
With children to come

We bet against the destruction
In store for us in underground silos.
We raise the glass, and rejoice.

September 24, 1983

Job Society

1.

Distraught, midnights
in a hot bath, anxious
and already weary
on awakening, neck

loaded with implosions
at my desk, nightmares
coming and going on
subways and buses, I

go over and back and
over this, in a blur
I give myself this
continual talking to:

small helpings of advice.
I say: the only thing
you can do now
is act

in the spirit of
contradiction: it hurts
you: where you are
flattered and brutalized

don't expect to be
anything but confused.
You will have to stay
and leave at the same time.

Preserve
what you have built
but build
toward an open future

they can't destroy: those
now in power over you
are already asking
you to join them

in the grand ballroom
at the banquet, to honor those
now in power over them.
And so on. The bill

won't be presented to you
until you get back to the office
on Monday: there
you will be asked to

seduce and demean
the new recruits, systematically:
the ones who must succeed
you. And if you do

you will grow
hopeless.
And if you refuse
you will pay the price.

So tell yourself: everyone's
hands get dirty.
And tell yourself: you at least
will withhold your consent

and get out.
So you tell yourself.
The only thing to do
is act in the spirit

of the contradictions
that hurt you.
Everywhere you look
there are only more jobs

like this one:
and all welded together
by material fear
and workplace autocracy.

2.

Or I ask myself, hating
the question: what can I be
in these wretched times?

The people I know
haven't held onto their seething
humanity

unless they made themselves
thick-skinned
persistent and time-rich

truculent under attack
and powered by the perspective
long memories give.

So I am always telling
myself—one is so short-lived
and intermittent—

Begin at once
to invent details of hope
for freedom, and persevere

in the one desire
they cannot satisfy:
in this way you will keep alive

the possibility of resistance
even as you serve the institution
that oppresses and feeds you.

Bad Air

where the knees were, suckholes
of bodily fluid

and you keep going the windows the walls the bannisters grabbed
by vertigo
the eight empty places
in the head
where the eyeballs and brains were
bedded on warmed
air turn to stone I am speaking
of what happens in a mild
to moderate attack

invisibility falls
through the air infiltrated by timebombs painlessly
deposited in each nostril
one breath at a time

two
gallons
of mucus pour down
the throat
(every 24 hours)

As the prevalence of sinusitis increases
voter turnout falls (off the air)
asleep at the table we are now interrupted by the CNN

war

these particle murders

these

if anyone asks me, I

or anyway used to

weakness of many
kinds I know what I have to say
sounds bizarre   I am

listening to the aura that's suddenly here and humming
over an enemy
that lifts the breathers of this place
off in a fever of prayer

January 23, 1991

Marc Kaminsky is a writer and psychotherapist. He has previously published five books of poems, including **The Road from Hiroshima, Daily Bread** and **A Table with People**. His books on the culture of aging include **The Uses of Reminiscence** and **What's Inside You It Shines Out of You,** a widely acclaimed work that initiated the practice of reminiscing and writing workshops with old people. His essays and poems have appeared in many magazines and anthologies. He has worked with The Open Theater, The Talking Band and Ballad Theater as writer-in-residence, collaborating (respectively) on **Terminal, Worksong,** and **In the Traffic of a Targeted City.**

He is currently at work on a multivolume series of cultural studies on storytelling and "the tradition of the oppressed" among Yiddish-speaking immigrants: this grew out of his collaboration with the anthropologist Barbara Myerhoff. He co-directs the Myerhoff Center at the YIVO Institute, and is in private practice in Brooklyn.